CITIZEN ENEMY

HOW MILITARIZED POLICE THREATEN CIVIL LIBERTIES

BY

THOMAS A. EMANUEL

Copyright

Copyright © 2014 by Emanuel Marketing. All Rights Reserved. This book or any portion thereof may not be reproduced or used in any manner whatsoever without the express written permission of Emanuel Marketing except for the use of brief quotations in a book review.

Printed in the United States of America.

First Printing, 2014.

ISBN-13: 978-1500898397

ISBN-10: 1500898392

FORWARD

We live in a time when the very existence of our Republic is at stake. When corruption is rampant, when the integrity of our institutions is at a critical low, when justice is but a fondly remembered dream and when our highest officials are beholden to strident self-interest, and when seemingly every one puts their own good ahead of that of the nation as a whole.

To a great extent our Republic is sick. It is rife with strife. Cooperation for the best interest of the people the politicians are supposed to represent is nearly moribund. While the special interests fight for a bigger and bigger piece of the pie, while the power hungry and the control freaks take away from the poor and the middle class even the little benefits that they have left, the great swath of Americans wonder why they should even care any more. They stay away from the polls in droves. They condemn the whole damn power structure to the lowest pit in hell. They are not far from complete despair or complete rebellion.

Those with just a glimmer of hope left write letters to their Congressman. They go to the polls and vote for another candidate who does not represent them, but only the moneyed interests who put him in power and keep him there at their pleasure. The "Occupy Wall Street" movement was a gasp of air from people who thought they could, maybe, bring attention to the ills within and bring about some slight change. It was brutally put down by police doing what they were told to do by the establishment. "None of that, boys, get those damn protestors off of our backs."

In the midst of all this uncaring bludgeoning of the poor and the middle class, the police have been militarized to an unbelievable extent. The power structure is well aware that mass rebellion is directly ahead if they keep up their addictive taking and never give anything, not even hope, to the 80% of people in the United States who are down to scrabbling through a miserable existence, getting by on pennies. They are going to need a police force who considers the public to be the enemy if they are to survive the massive public hatred they are creating.

How did we get to this sick state of the Republic? We hope to touch on some of that here.

DEADLY FORCE

There are very dangerous armed thugs walking the streets of every city and town in the United States today. The average citizen cannot call the police to protect themselves from these thugs because these thugs <u>are </u>the police!

Let's take a look at the gradual deterioration of police psychology and the development of the siege mentality among police agencies to the point where they actually consider the people they 'serve" to be the enemy. For that we need to step back a little. We need to get some perspective, an understanding of where policing came from and how it has moved into the dreadful state that it is in today.

Do I mean to say that all police agencies are corrupted, filled with macho idiots who think they can beat up citizens and kill them for no cause, but simply because they can get away with it? Of course not! There are a great many fine officers working in a tough unrewarding job with benefits that do not outweigh the hazards they face on a daily basis. But, as usual, the bad apples give a very bad name to the good work of caring and lawfully respectful officers. Unfortunately the bad apples in this basket are not just a few. They are becoming, at least in the minds of a growing majority of U.S. citizens, the norm. Citizens, especially black citizens, are scared of the police like never before, and they are tremendously and rightfully angry at police policies in their communities.

So let's take a hard look at policing and how it has evolved in America.

Historically policing has always arisen from and been part of the community in which it operates in the United States. Here is a quote from "The History of Police" by Sage Publications (www.sagepub.com/upm-data/50819_ch_1.pdf footnotes redacted):

"American policing has been heavily influenced by the English system throughout the course of history. In the early stages of development in both England and Colonial America, citizens were responsible for law enforcement in their communities. The English referred to this as *kin police* in which people were responsible for watching out for their relatives or kin.

Section 1 **The History of the Police.** In Colonial America, a watch system consisting of citizen volunteers (usually men) was in place until the mid-19th century. Citizens that were part of watch groups provided social services, including lighting street lamps, running soup kitchens, recovering lost children, capturing runaway animals, and a variety of other services; their involvement in crime control activities at this time was minimal at best. Policing in England and Colonial America was largely ineffective, as it was based on a volunteer system and their method of patrol was both disorganized and sporadic.

Sometime later, the responsibility of enforcing laws shifted from individual citizen volunteers to groups of men living within the community; this was referred to as the **frankpledge system** in England. The frankpledge system was a semistructured system in which groups of men were responsible for enforcing the law. Men living within a community would form groups of 10 called **tythings** (or tithings); tythings were then grouped into *hundreds*, and then hundreds were grouped into *shires* (similar to counties). A person called the *shire reeve* (sheriff) was then chosen to be in charge of each shire. The individual members of tythings were responsible for capturing criminals and bringing them to court, while shire reeves were responsible for providing a number of services, including the oversight of the activities conducted by the tythings in their shire.

A similar system existed in America during this time in which constables, sheriffs, and citizen-based watch groups were responsible for policing in the colonies. Sheriffs were responsible for catching criminals, working with the courts, and collecting taxes; law enforcement was not a top priority for sheriffs, as they could make more money by collecting taxes within the community. Night watch groups in Colonial America, as well as day watch groups that were added at a later time, were largely ineffective; instead of controlling crime in their community, some members of the watch groups would sleep and/or socialize while they were on duty. These citizen-based watch groups were not equipped to deal with the increasing social unrest and rioting that were beginning to occur in both England and Colonial America in the late 1700s through the early 1800s. It was at this point in time that publicly funded police departments began to emerge across both England and Colonial America."

And later things changed again with the professionalization of policing in the U.S. Here is another quote from the same source (www.sagepub.com/upm-data/50819_ch_1.pdf again footnotes redacted):

"Policing Reform in the United States (1900s–1970s)

Political involvement in American policing was viewed as a problem by both the public and police reformers in the mid- to late 19th century. Early attempts (in the 19th century) at police reform in the United States were unsuccessful, as citizens tried to pressure police agencies to make changes. Later on in the early 20th century (with help from the Progressives), reform efforts began to take hold and made significant changes to policing in the United States.

A goal of police reform included the removal of politics from American policing. This effort included the creation of standards for recruiting and hiring police officers and administrators instead of allowing politicians to appoint these individuals to help them carry out their political agendas.

Another goal of police reform during the early 1900s was to professionalize the police. This could be achieved by setting standards for the quality of police officers hired, implementing better police training, and adopting various types of technology to aid police officers in their daily operations (including motorized patrol and the use of two-way radios). The professionalization movement of the police in America resulted in police agencies becoming centralized bureaucracies focused primarily on crime control. The importance of the role of "crime fighter" was highlighted in the Wickersham Commission report (1931), which examined rising crime rates in the United States and the inability of the police to manage this problem. It was proposed in this report that police officers could more effectively deal with rising crime by focusing their police duties primarily on crime control instead of the social services that they had once provided in the political era."

Please notice that the rising crime rates occurred in middle of the great depression when the populace as a whole was suffering lack of employment, hunger, and poverty brought on by the excesses of stock speculation and money manipulation. Sound familiar to the depression caused by Wall Street at the end of the Bush Administration?

Today this historical community-based policing system has largely disappeared in 21st century America. Police departments are much more professional, technical, and scientific. The officers often don't come from communities they work in. And when they do they are often selected based on other criteria than their ability to relate to the community.

As a result there is a very pervasive attitude in police departments of it's us against them. We are the righteous and the true. We represent, believe in, and assure law and order. Our officers do not do wrong and commit crimes. They do what they have to do to keep order and preserve peace. This attitude is commonly expressed in the inability of police agencies to control corruption and abuse within their own ranks. An officer does not "rat" on his fellow officers. He sees his fellow officers as an integral part of his existence and his safety, both physical and psychological. Everyone else is an outsider to that critical relationship, and perhaps antagonistic toward the police themselves. This mode of thinking is very important in the life and death situations faced on a daily basis by police officers. Your brother officer has your back.

Since the 1970's two radical changes have occurred in policing. These attitudinal changes of stunning proportions have occurred over about a forty year time period in this country.

In the 70's and 80's police philosophy was one of professionalism rooted in the ethic of "to protect and serve". This basically meant that the police were on the side of the community against the menace of the criminal. Police had a mindset of protecting the public, living by the motto "to serve and protect". This essentially meant that the public, through their elected representatives, the mayor and the city council, was the boss. The police officer was your friend and the hero who protected the community from everything illegal or immoral, starting with petty theft and white collar crime all the way through murder and mayhem. They acted on your behalf to protect you and yours while you were able to go on with your life, hopefully to grow and prosper.

The first big change was the phenomenon of people actually attacking police. Except in the very rare case of escaped convicts or organized crime, the police were not attacked. Criminals tended to avoid the police as much as possible, to conduct their illegal activities in secret, and to attempt to get away with it without suffering the consequences. The police were on the side of the community and the community actively and whole-heartedly backed the police. This, of course, was truer in white communities than in communities dominated by people of color. But nevertheless it was generally true throughout the United States.

Police forces have always dealt with life and death situations, but the circumstances surrounding the taking of a life have drastically changed. In the early 1980's a trend began to be recognized that we now label "suicide by cop". It has even been formally defined.

Here is the definition. A person who is intent on suicide realizes that police officers will use deadly force in certain situations. He sets up the confrontation in a way that will provoke the police into killing him. He points a gun at an officer or an innocent bystander and it results in the officer firing in self defense or to protect the innocent. The perpetrator is killed and the officer comes under investigation.

Or the suicide has been known to attack an officer with a knife, try to run an officer down with a car, or attempt to set off a bomb. Criminals who refused to surrender when cornered by the police and fire upon the police, drawing return fire, are going to inevitably end their life in a hail of police bullets. The overwhelming majority of these cases were men who fought it out with the police. Females rarely, if ever, participated in this brand of idiocy.

When the police were forced into shooting people the use of deadly force became much more common. Police deaths also happened at a very uncomfortable rate. Then two things happened in the psychology of policing.

First the job became much more dangerous causing a series of emotional responses among serving officers. The concept of us against the community became more strongly engrained, when as an officer you never knew when you would encounter a suspect who would fight until one of you was dead. Policing became an activity in which you might have to put your life on the line every day when you went to work. Trust in the community greatly eroded among peace officers.

Secondly, the value of a human life was cheapened immeasurably. Remember this was just after the country went through the horrendous upheaval and unrest of the Vietnam War. Life was cheapened overseas during that war when soldiers fought against civilians in pajamas; the entire Vietnamese population was suspect, and when military excesses like Mai Lai took place. Many police officers were veterans and had experienced these life threatening conditions in which deadly force could be brought against you from anywhere in your environment. Some of that wariness and mistrust of your community and your environment naturally seeped into the police community.

The next evolution of deadly force was a sea change and it effected every single police department in whole country. Wikipedia details the events in Los Angeles in February of 1997 (http://en.wikipedia.org/wiki/North_Hollywood_shootout)

"On the morning of Friday, February 28, 1997, after months of preparation, including extensive reconnoitering of their intended target—the Bank of America branch located at 6600 Laurel Canyon Boulevard—Phillips and Mătăsăreanu loaded five rifles and approximately 3,300 rounds of ammunition in box and drum magazines into the trunk of their vehicle: two converted fully automatic Norinco Type 56 S rifles, a converted fully automatic Norinco Type 56 S-1, a semi automatic HK-91, and converted fully automatic Bushmaster (M16) XM15 Dissipator.[16] They filled a jam jar with gasoline and placed it in the back seat with the intention of setting the car and weapons on fire to destroy evidence after the robbery. Phillips wore roughly 40 lbs of equipment, including a Type IIIA bulletproof vest and groin guard, a load bearing vest and multiple military canteen pouches for ammunition storage, and several pieces of home made body armor created from spare vests, covering his shins, thighs, and forearms.[17] Mătăsăreanu wore only a Type IIIA bulletproof vest, but included a metal trauma plate to protect vital organs. Additionally, both robbers had sewn watch faces onto the back of their gloves to check their timing inside the bank.[18] Before entering, they took the barbiturate phenobarbital, prescribed to Mătăsăreanu as an anticonvulsant, to calm their nerves.[19]

The robbery

Phillips and Mătăsăreanu, driving a white 1987 Chevrolet Celebrity, arrived at the Bank of America branch office at the intersection of Laurel Canyon Boulevard and Archwood Street in North Hollywood around 9:17 AM, and set their watch alarms for eight minutes, the police response time they had estimated. To come up with this timeframe, Phillips had used a radio scanner to monitor police transmissions prior to the robbery.[19] But as the two were walking in, they were spotted by two Los Angeles police officers, Loren Farrell and Martin Perello, who were driving down Laurel Canyon in a patrol car. Officer Perello issued a call on the radio, "15-A-43, requesting assistance, we have a possible 211 in progress at the Bank of America." 211 is the code for an armed robbery.[20]

As they entered the bank, Phillips and Mătăsăreanu forced a customer leaving the ATM lobby near the entrance into the bank and onto the floor. A security guard inside saw the scuffle and the heavily armed robbers and radioed his partner in the parking lot to call the police; the call was not received. Phillips shouted "This is a fucking hold up!"[21] before he and Mătăsăreanu opened fire into the ceiling to in an attempt scare the approximately thirty bank staff and customers[2] and to discourage resistance.[22] Mătăsăreanu shot open the bulletproof door (it was designed to resist only small-caliber rounds) and gained access to the tellers and vault. The robbers forced assistant manager John Villigrana to open the vault. Villigrana obliged and began to fill the robbers' money bag. However, due to a change in the bank's delivery schedule, the vault contained significantly less than the $750,000 the gunmen had expected. Mătăsăreanu, seemingly enraged at this development, argued with Villigrana and demanded more. In an apparent show of frustration, Mătăsăreanu then fired a full drum magazine of 75 rounds into the bank's safe, destroying much of the remaining money. In the end, the two would leave with $303,305.[15]

The shootout

Outside, the first-responding officers heard gunfire from the bank and made another radio call for additional units before taking cover behind their patrol car, weapons trained on the bank doors. While the robbers were still inside, more patrol and detective units arrived and took strategic positions at all four corners of the bank, effectively surrounding it. At approximately 9:32 AM, Phillips exited through the north doorway and briefly looked around, possibly to survey the positions of police. Officers shouted repeatedly for Phillips to drop his weapon and surrender, but he turned around and walked back inside. Several minutes later, he reemerged from the north doorway, while Mătăsăreanu exited through the south.[23]

Phillips and Mătăsăreanu began to engage the officers, firing sporadic bursts into the patrol cars that had been positioned on Laurel Canyon in front of the bank.[16] Officers immediately returned fire. The patrol officers were armed with standard Beretta 92F and Beretta 92FS 9mm pistols and Smith & Wesson Model 15 .38 caliber revolvers, while officers including James Zaboravan also carried a 12-gauge Ithaca Model 37 pump-action shotgun. The officers' weaponry could not penetrate aramid body armor worn by Phillips and Mătăsăreanu, which covered most of their bodies and provided more bullet resistance than standard-issue police Kevlar vests. The robbers' heads were the only vital organs that were unprotected, but most of the LAPD officers' service pistols had insufficient range and poor accuracy at long distances.[15] Additionally, the officers were pinned down by the heavy spray of gunfire coming from the robbers, making it difficult to attempt a headshot.

Multiple officers and civilians were wounded in the seven to eight minutes from when the shooting began to when Mătăsăreanu entered the robbers' white sedan to make a getaway. By this time, television news helicopters were arriving on the scene. SWAT commanders would use the live coverage to pass critical, time-sensitive information to officers on the ground. Mătăsăreanu ushered Phillips to get into the vehicle, but Phillips remained outside of it, retrieved a HK-91 from the trunk, and continued firing on officers and helicopters while crouching behind the cars in the parking lot. As Phillips approached the driver side of getaway vehicle after suppressing officers, a shotgun blast hit him above the left wrist. In response, Phillips quickly backed away from the vehicle and continued firing, holding the rifle with his injured forearm against the magwell. Phillips fired roughly 60 to 120 rounds from the HK-91 until it was struck in the receiver and magazine by police bullets. He later retrieved a Norinco Type 56 S-1 from the trunk of the Celebrity.[15]

SWAT arrives

After LAPD radio operators received the second "officer down" call from police at the shootout, a tactical alert was issued. The SWAT team arrived 18 minutes after the shooting had begun. They were armed with AR-15s, and wore running shoes and shorts under their body armor, as they had been on an exercise run when they received the call. Upon arrival, they commandeered a nearby armored truck, which was used to extract wounded civilians and officers from the scene.[15]

Deaths of the gunmen

At 9:52, Phillips, who had been using the getaway vehicle as cover, split from Mătăsăreanu. Turning east on Archwood Street, he took cover behind a parked truck and continued to fire at the police until his rifle jammed.[24] He attempted to clear the jam but ultimately discarded the weapon, drew a Beretta 92FS pistol, and continued firing at police. He was then shot in the right hand, causing him to drop the pistol. After retrieving it, he placed the muzzle under his chin and fired. As his body fell, a bullet struck the back of his neck, severing his spine.[citation needed] Officers across the street continued to engage Phillips with several additional shots while on the ground. After the firing had stopped, officers in the area surrounded Phillips, cuffed him, and removed his ski mask. It is speculated that his death was accidental; being unable to pull back the slide of the Beretta with his injured hand, he attempted to do so with his teeth, and the gun unintentionally discharged.[citation needed]

Mătăsăreanu's vehicle was rendered nearly inoperable after its tires were shot out.[15] At 9:56, he attempted to carjack a yellow 1963 Jeep Gladiator pickup truck on Archwood, three blocks east of where Phillips died, and transferred all of his weapons and ammunition from the getaway car into the truck.[25] However, sources say Mătăsăreanu was unable to start the truck, because the driver had turned the vehicle and fuel pumps off, leaving the keys in the ignition.[26] Others say that it was because the driver had taken the keys with him after fleeing the car.[25] As KCBS and KCAL helicopters hovered overhead, a patrol car driven by SWAT officers quickly arrived. Mătăsăreanu left the truck, took cover behind the original getaway car, and engaged them for 2 1/2 minutes of almost uninterrupted gunfire. Mătăsăreanu's chest armor deflected a double tap from one of the SWAT officers, but it briefly winded him. After several seconds he continued firing. At least one SWAT officer fired his AR-15 below the cars and wounded Mătăsăreanu in his unprotected lower legs; he was soon unable to continue and put his hands up to show surrender.[15] Seconds after his defeat, officers swarmed him to pin him down. As he was being cuffed, SWAT officers asked for his name, to which he replied "Pete". When asked if there were any more suspects, he reportedly retorted "Fuck you! Shoot me in the head!".[27] The police radioed for an ambulance, but Mătăsăreanu, loudly swearing profusely and still goading the police to shoot him, died before the ambulance could reach the scene almost seventy minutes later. Later reports showed that Mătăsăreanu was shot over 20 times in the legs and died from trauma due to excessive blood loss coming from 2 gunshot wounds in his left thigh.[28]

Most of the incident, including the death of Phillips and the death of Mătăsăreanu, was broadcast live by news helicopters, which hovered over the scene and televised the action as events unfolded.[16] Over 300 law enforcement officers from various forces had responded to the city-wide TAC alert.[29] By the time the shooting had stopped, Phillips and Mătăsăreanu had fired about 1,100 rounds, approximately a round every two seconds.[15]"

This incredibly violent crime scene was a shock to the whole nation. But to the entire law enforcement community it was a total awakening to a completely different new world! Two lousy criminals, common bank robbers no less, were better equipped and more capable than almost an entire police force.

They had automatic weapons, bullet proof vests, and more ammunition by far than the police.

This could NOT be allowed to stand. The criminals could not be allowed to out gun the police. Not in America. Maybe this is was what happened in places like Columbia where the cartels killed the good guys and ran the country. But, by God, in America we are going to have law and order!

In the meantime other significant developments were taking place. In 1990 the Congress enacted a law as part of the National Defense Authorization Act for that year. This act is part of the standard appropriations enacted every year to keep the government running. But this time something new was included. It was a program called the 1033. The program is managed by the Department of Defense and sends surplus military equipment to State and local police departments. Until 1996 the law specified that this material was to be used only for interdiction of drug related activities, but in that year it was authorized for use in both anti-drug and anti-terrorism activities.

But from the shock wave set off in 1997, when police departments around the country realized that they could be outgunned, the demand for military style equipment, tactics, and training has been ever increasing. The 1033 program fulfilled a lot of the perceived police need.

The attack on the United States on 9/11/2011 did not help the situation. The massive response against terrorism was certainly justified, but it trickled down to State and local agencies in a way that began to turn police departments into what some have likened to occupying forces.

The 1033 program has grown apace. The Pentagon has distributed over 400 mine-resistant armored vehicles (mine resistant !!) to local police departments. It has also given them a significant number of other armored vehicles. Police agencies have also acquired hundreds of aircraft, and close to 100,000 assault rifles.

This material is all free of charge to State and local police agencies. If you are the local police chief and your officers come to you and say, "Chief, our brothers in the next county have all these goodies from DOD. What about us? Don't we need that equipment too, just in case?" What are you going to do? Are you going to say, "No, I'm sorry, but that stuff is only for the military. We are police and we have a totally different mission and reason for existence." Actually you probably would say, "Lets get all we can."

And so, feeling threatened by the violence of the society in which they operate, and knowing that their neighbors are armed to the teeth with guns and even assault rifles, and that many in their communities are gun nuts, the police armored up. Why not? It's free and they might need it someday.

This was all happening despite the fact that violent crime has dropped precipitously over the last 20 years. According to the FBI in 1993 in the U.S. there were 747.1 violent crimes per 100,000 population, but by 2012 that number had dropped to 386.9. (http://www.fbi.gov/about-us/cjis/ucr/crime-in-the-u.s/2012/crime-in-the-u.s.-2012/tables/1tabledatadecoverviewpdf/table_1_crime_in_the_united_states_by_volume_and_rate_per_100000_inhabitants_1993-2012.xls)

Maybe, some would say, that is because the police are better armed. That is an unlikely explanation, however, because most violent crime is robbery, assault, rape and murder which has very little to do with the weaponry actually possessed by the criminals. Their weapons tend to be fists, knives, and handguns.

FROM PROTECTION TO ATTACK

So at this point we have police agencies all across the country heavily armed with military equipment. They are on high alert because terrorism in the United States has come to be a reality, when most of our lives we never truly believed it could happen here. It creates paranoia. And they are facing a population which is more heavily armed by far than any other in the world.

According to the Small Arms Survey, an independent research project based in Geneva, Switzerland, in 2014 there are 97 guns for every one hundred people in the United States including every man, woman and child. This is more than double the amount which exists even in war torn countries like Iraq, Yemen, and Serbia. It is really an insane situation.

Police officers are trained to be aggressive and to be in control. There has to be some control. And police departments are all about control like no other kind of entity. When officers are out on the streets or responding to calls they are trained to take control of the situation and to brook no opposition. They are the authority and that authority is absolute and to be instantly obeyed.

This flies in the face of reality, of course, and it also tramples all over civil rights like freedom of speech, freedom of assembly, and freedom from unreasonable search and seizure. But police attitudes seem to be to shoot first and ask questions later. That is where it really gets out of hand.

The police are now the ones committing homicide. Every single day there is a story in the papers or on the news of police killing an innocent citizen. These homicidal tendencies are very far from being uncommon. They seem to be getting worse all the time and the police seem to want to shoot civilians under the most trivial of circumstances. Let's just detail some examples here so you can realize the trend.

It can be very dangerous, not to mention life threatening, to go shopping and handle a toy gun today. A 22 year old man found that out recently and did not live to tell about it, as reported by Nisha Chittal (http://www.msnbc.com/msnbc/cops-shoot-and-kill-man-holding-toy-gun-walmart)

"A young man holding a toy rifle in a Wal-Mart was shot and killed on Tuesday by police in the Dayton suburb of Beavercreek, Ohio, according to Raw Story. John Crawford, 22, was carrying a toy gun he picked up in the store, alarming two other shoppers.

LeeCee Johnson, the mother of Crawford's children, told the *Dayton Daily News* she was on the phone with him while he was browsing in the store. "We was just talking," she told the Ohio newspaper. "He said he was at the video games playing videos and he went over there by the toy section where the toy guns were. And the next thing I know, he said 'It's not real,' and the police start shooting and they said 'Get on the ground,' but he was already on the ground because they had shot him. And I could hear him just crying and screaming. I feel like they shot him down like he was not even human."

CBS reports that two other Wal-Mart customers, April and Ronald Ritchie, saw Crawford walking around the store with what appeared to be a gun and called the police. The police station reports that officers asked Crawford to put down the weapon, and opened fire when he did not comply. He later died of his gun shot wounds at a nearby hospital, where his death was ruled a homicide by the Montgomery County coroner's office. A request for comment by msnbc to the Beavercreek police department was not immediately returned.

The Ohio Attorney General's office has said that the gun Crawford was carrying was an MK-177 BB/Pellet rifle, also known as a "variable pump air rifle." Family members could not be reached for comment by msnbc.

Tasha Thomas, who identified herself as Crawford's girlfriend, told the *Dayton Daily News* that she drove Crawford to the Wal-Mart and was also in the store, but was in a different aisle from Crawford when the shooting happened. He was not armed when he entered the store, she said. "He did not have any type of gun on him. It's not fair."

A relative told the paper the family had contacted the NAACP and the National Action Network, a civil rights group led by MSNBC's Rev. Al Sharpton."

In this case there may have been some pretext for taking deadly action. The kid was holding a "gun" and although he said it was not real criminals lie all the time. Maybe he was lying when he said it was not real.

Was mortal force justified? In my view it was not. The cops said they ordered him to drop the gun and he didn't so they shot him. Apparently he had no clue as to why the police where there and he knew he was not doing anything wrong so he replied that it was not real. He did not instantaneously comply with their orders, so they shot him. No explanations are acceptable. Obey immediately, no matter the circumstances, or die. No presumption of innocence. No quarter given. This is a battlefield and in battle you do not give the enemy the chance to kill you first.

Was this kid "the enemy"? In the minds of the cops apparently he was. But this is America, the land of the free and the home of the brave, not a war zone.

Let's take another example. Across the country in Homer, Louisiana an incident was reported by Howard Witt, a reporter for the Chicago Tribune (http://articles.latimes.com/2009/mar/17/nation/na-race-shootings17)

"HOMER, La.—On the last afternoon of his life, Bernard Monroe was hosting a cookout for family and friends in front of his dilapidated home on Adams Street in this small northern Louisiana town.

Throat cancer had robbed the 73-year-old retired electric utility worker of his voice years ago, but family members said Monroe was clearly enjoying the commotion of a dozen of his grandchildren and great-grandchildren cavorting around him in the dusty, grassless yard.

Then the Homer police showed up, two white officers whose arrival caused the participants at the black family gathering to quickly fall silent.

Within moments, Monroe lay dead, shot by one of the officers as his family looked on.

Now the Louisiana State Police, the FBI and the U.S. Justice Department are swarming over this impoverished lumber town of

3,800, drawn by the allegations of numerous witnesses that police killed an unarmed, elderly black man without justification—and then moved a gun to make it look like the man had been holding it.

"We are closely monitoring the events in Homer," said Donald Washington, the U.S. attorney for the Western District of Louisiana. "I understand that a number of allegations are being made that, if true, would be serious enough for us to follow up on very quickly."
………

"All the anecdotal information demonstrates that African Americans are the most frequent victims of zealous, inappropriate police activity that often winds up in a shooting," said Reggie Shuford, a senior attorney with the racial justice program at the American Civil Liberties Union. "It's a shoot first, ask questions later approach to policing."

The evidence is not merely anecdotal. The most recent national analysis from the Justice Department's Bureau of Justice Statistics shows that blacks and Hispanics were nearly three times as likely as whites to be searched by police—and blacks were almost four times as likely as whites to be subjected to the use of force.

Psychologists are stepping up research into the implicit, unconscious racial biases that may be driving such statistics and affecting police behavior.

"If in fact police have implicit biases—if they automatically associate blacks with crime—then that would be relevant to an officer in a split-second, shoot-or-don't-shoot situation," said Lorie Fridell, a criminology professor at the University of South Florida who is creating a new anti-bias police training program with funding from the Justice Department. "Is the officer more inclined to believe he sees a gun in the hand of a black person, rather than a cell phone? I think that is possible."

In Monroe's case, friends and family members say they still don't understand why the beloved neighborhood patriarch ended up dead.

Four witnesses told the Tribune that Monroe was sitting outside his home in the late afternoon of Feb. 20, clutching a large sports-drink bottle, when two police officers pulled up and summoned Monroe's son, Shawn, for a conversation.

Shawn Monroe has a long record of arrests and convictions for assault and battery, and even though he was not wanted on any current warrants, he took off running into the house. One of the officers, a new hire named Tim Cox who had been on Homer's police force for only a few weeks, chased after him, reappearing moments later in the doorway.

Meanwhile, the witnesses said, the elder Monroe had started walking toward the front door, carrying only his drink bottle, to try to intervene. When Monroe got to the first step on the front porch, the witnesses said, Cox opened fire, striking him several times as adults and children stood nearby.

"He just shot him through the screen door," said Denise Nicholson, a family friend who said she was standing a few feet from Monroe. "After [Monroe] was on the ground, we kept asking the officer to call an ambulance, but all he did was get on his radio and say, 'Officer in distress.' "

As Monroe lay dying, the witnesses said, the second police officer, who has not been publicly identified, picked up a handgun that Monroe, an avid hunter, always kept in plain sight on the porch for protection. Using a police-issue blue latex glove, the officer grasped the gun by its handle, the witnesses said, and then ordered everyone to back away from the scene. The next thing they said they saw was the gun on the ground next to Monroe's body.

"I saw him pick up the gun off the porch," said Marcus Frazier, another witness. "I said, 'What are you doing?' The cop told me, 'Shut the hell up, you don't know what you're talking about.' "

The Homer police maintain that Monroe was holding a loaded gun when he was shot, but they are not commenting further on the case.

At least one fact surrounding the shooting is not in dispute: It took place amid long-standing tensions between Homer police and the residents of Monroe's crime-plagued black neighborhood.

"People here are afraid of the police," said Terry Willis, vice president of the Homer NAACP branch. "They harass black people, they stop people for no reason and rough them up without charging them with anything."

That is how it should be, responded Russell Mills, Homer's police chief, who noted the high rates of gun and drug arrests in the neighborhood.

"If I see three or four young black men walking down the street, I have to stop them and check their names," said Mills, who is white. "I want them to be afraid every time they see the police that they might get arrested. We're not out there trying to abuse and harass people—we're trying to protect the law-abiding citizens locked behind their doors in fear."

hwitt@tribune.com Copyright © 2014, Chicago Tribune"

This is a much more egregious case than that of the kid in the shopping mall with a toy gun. Here the police had no reason whatsoever to suspect that Mr. Monroe was a threat in any way. And then they tried to justify the murder by planting false evidence of a gun in his hand in full view of other witnesses. On top of that the Homer police chief thinks that this is all fine and dandy and that fear of the police and murder by the police "is how it should be". That is plain and unmitigated abuse of law enforcement authority. The police chief defends his officer's actions no matter how stupid, disastrous or illegal they may be. That is wrong, totally wrong, and cannot be accepted or tolerated.

You may think this is pretty bad and that there is no justification for killing somebody with a water bottle in his hand. And worse, the officers attempted to plant "evidence" to justify the killing or mitigate the actions of the officers.

Well, it actually gets worse. Wikipedia carries this incident detailing the murder of Kelly Thomas in Fullerton, California.(http://en.wikipedia.org/wiki/Death_of_Kelly_Thomas)

"On July 5, 2011, at about 8:30 PM, officers of the Fullerton Police Department responded to a call from the management of the Slidebar[20] that someone was vandalizing cars near the Fullerton Transportation Center. While investigating, they encountered the shirtless and disheveled Thomas and attempted to search him. According to statements given by the officers, Thomas was uncooperative and resisted when they attempted to search him, so backup was called.[21] "Now you see my fists?" Fullerton police officer Manny Ramos asked Thomas while slipping on a pair of latex gloves. "Yeah, what about them?" Thomas responded. "They are getting ready to fuck you up," said Ramos. A video of the event surfaced, and Thomas can be heard repeatedly screaming in pain while officers are heard repeatedly asking him to place his arms behind his back. He audibly responds "Okay, I'm sorry!" and "I'm trying!" while the officers stretch his arm back. The police officers claim that, unable to get Thomas to comply with the requests, they used a taser on him (up to five times according to a witness statement, and the video footage), and in the video Thomas can be heard screaming "Dad! Dad!".[22] Six officers were involved in subduing Thomas, who was unarmed and had a history of mental illness. Thomas was initially taken to St. Jude Medical Center in Fullerton but was transferred immediately to the UC Irvine Medical Center with severe injuries to his head, face, and neck.[23] One of the paramedics testified that he was first instructed to attend to a police officer's minor injury and then noticed Thomas lying unconscious in a pool of blood.[24][25]

Orange County District Attorney Tony Rackauckas gave a detailed account of the events during a press conference on September 21,

2011. Using digital audio recording devices carried by the officers, surveillance video from a pole camera on YouTube at the Fullerton Transportation Center, and other evidence, Rackauckas provided evidence that Thomas did comply with orders from Officer Ramos, who had put on latex gloves and asked Thomas "Now see my fists? They are getting ready to fuck you up."[26] Rackauckas went on to describe how Thomas begged for his life, before being struck repeatedly by the officers. He was admitted to the hospital, slipped into a coma, and died five days later.

Medical records show that bones in his face were broken and he choked on his own blood.[4] The coroner concluded that compression of the thorax made it impossible for Thomas to breathe normally and deprived his brain of oxygen.[5] His parents removed him from life support five days later, and he died from his injuries on July 10, 2011.[6] Officer Manuel Ramos was charged with one count of second-degree murder and one count of involuntary manslaughter; Corporal Jay Cicinelli and Officer Joseph Wolfe were each charged with one count of felony involuntary manslaughter and one count of excessive force.[5][7][8] All three pleaded not guilty.

A judge declined to dismiss the charges against the officers in January 2013, finding that "a reasonable person could infer that the use of force was excessive and unreasonable."[9] An appeals court judge also denied a request to overturn the lower court's decision.[10] On January 13, 2014, Ramos and Cicinelli were found not guilty of all charges,[11] while the trial for Joe Wolfe was pending.[12] Following the verdict for the two officers, the district attorney's office announced it would not pursue the case against Officer Wolfe.[13] "

Police murder. No question about it. Police murder was condoned by a jury who acquitted the murderers of all charges. This is not policing. This is total abuse of power. These are criminals and thugs wearing the trappings of legal authority. It reduces society to the laws of the jungle.

You will notice that in the cases cited here there is increasing violence on the part of the police and decreasing evidence of any reason why deadly force should have been used. In the first case, John Crawford, the 22 year old was carrying a gun, but it was a toy gun. In the second case, Mr. Monroe, had no weapon and was not attacking the police in any way. The police tried to fabricate "evidence" that would be a justification as to their reason for killing him. But it was crude and callous and done right in front of his family. In the third case, Kelly Thomas was homeless and mentally deranged and just happened to be in wrong place. He had absolutely nothing to do with the crime being investigated and was beaten to death for no reason. The officers went to trial and were acquitted. They did not even try to pretend that he was a threat to them. He was a citizen and therefore "the enemy" and they summarily executed him.

Unfortunately none of these incidents are unusual in any way. They are happening on a daily basis all over America. USA Today reports that FBI statistics show that more than 400 police murders are committed each year. But the numbers are definitely under reported because only 750 police agencies of the more than 17,000 in the country participate in the reporting. The reporting is also voluntary.

Geoff Alpert is a criminologist at the University of South Carolina. Alpert, who has long studied police use of deadly force, said the FBI's limited database underscores a gaping hole in the nation's understanding of how often local police take a life on America's streets — and under what circumstances.
(http://www.usatoday.com/story/news/nation/2014/08/14/police-killings-data/14060357/)

"There is no national database for this type of information, and that is so crazy," said Alpert. "We've been trying for years, but nobody wanted to fund it and the (police) departments didn't want it. They were concerned with their image and liability. They don't want to bother with it."

At this writing we are in the midst of the Ferguson, Missouri case where an unarmed 18 year old black man, Michael Brown, was shot six times by police in full military combat gear. An independent autopsy showed that the shot that killed him went through the top of his skull. Michael Brown seems to have been killed because he was jay walking. The police ordered him to get up onto the sidewalk, which he did. Then he raised both hands above his head and Officer Darren Wilson shot him. Officer Wilson has not been arrested and the Ferguson police have attempted to disparage Michael Brown's character claiming he was involved in a robbery at a local store and there was evidence of marijuana in his system. Neither of these facts, even if they were true, have anything to do with why Michael Brown was killed.

This incident seems to have stemmed totally from racial prejudice and hatred. Ferguson police are almost totally white. There are only 3 black officers out of a total police force of 56 officers in this predominately black suburb of St. Louis. The small town of Ferguson is 67% African-American. Ferguson police have been heard calling demonstrators "fucking animals" and have even attacked and arrested members of the press for exercising their rights in filming or gathering information about the Brown murder and the subsequent protests.

This is a new and terrifying prospect which has emerged of police murdering unarmed citizens who are not threatening the police, and in fact are often begging them not to kill them. The African-American communities have bourne the vast majority of these killings and racial prejudice is clearly a major motivating factor in a large majority of these cases. There have also been many cases where someone who was defenseless or in some way not well protected by the powers that be, for example the homeless and mentally impaired Kelly Thomas, have been the victims.

Police violence in black communities is not new. But what is new is the unrepentant and barefaced nature of the murders in full public view and awareness.

Case after case of citizens being shot down by squads of heavily armed police forces in riot gear have shown up in large cities and small towns alike all across America. These squads show up at scenes where the force used by the authorities is out of all proportion to the threat to the public good, or the need for police in riot gear is minimal to non-existent in the minds of any reasonable observer.

In the wake of the Ferguson shooting more and more information has come out about police murder, about the 1033 program, and about the blatant abuse by police of citizens who are exercising their constitutional rights. Senators on both sides of the aisle, namely Senators Elizabeth Warren and Rand Paul, have condemned these police practices, called for cessation of the 1033 program and for police reform. But one thing is now totally clear:

The police consider the citizens of this country to be the enemy.

A SICK COUNTRY

It is an acknowledged fact that the population of entire countries can become psychologically sick.

It has happened most famously in Germany which spawned the Holocaust. The nation was completely intimidated by the Nazis, the Brown Shirts, and the type of criminal activities like *Kristallnacht* conducted by the country's authorities. On the night of the 9th of November 1938 "Crystal Night" occurred. The Brown Shirt police went berserk in almost all large German cities, and many small towns. They broke store windows in all the Jewish shops. Jewish houses and apartments were smashed, and synagogues were demolished and set on fire. Jews were arrested, beaten, and some were even killed. It was a horrendous, shameful event. But it is critical to realize that it was conducted in name of the authorities who ruled the country. The Jews were the ones who suffered that night, but in the long run the greatest harm was done to Germany and the German people. The nation ultimately had to suffer its total destruction in order to defeat this national sickness, called Nazism.

It happened in Japan during World War II when the entire nation was taken over by the cult of the Emperor. Wikipedia (http://en.wikipedia.org/wiki/Emperor_of_Japan) relates that:

"The role of the emperor as head of the State Shinto religion was exploited during the war, creating an Imperial cult that led to kamikaze bombers and other fanaticism. This in turn led to the requirement in the Potsdam Declaration for the elimination "for all time [of] the authority and influence of those who have deceived and misled the people of Japan into embarking on world conquest". Following Japan's surrender, the Allies issued the Shinto Directive separating church and state within Japan, leading to the Humanity Declaration of the incumbent Emperor. Subsequently, a new constitution was drafted to define the role of the emperor and the government."

In other words Japan had to be completely redefined constitutionally, after it was conquered, in order to restore sanity to the nation and to bring it back into the family of civilized nations conducting its affairs in harmony with other nation states.

It would be well for us to remember that mania and triumphalism has brought other great civilizations to disaster. The writings of the Greek historian Thucydides described how the power madness of the Athenians in the 5th Century BC caused their downfall. The Athenians along with their Greek allies won a decisive naval battle at Salamis over a much larger fleet possessed by the Persians. Then they formed a League with the other Greek city-states in 477 B.C. on the island of Delos. In time the Athenians dominated this alliance by providing most of the ships and men, while the other city-states sent money. Soon the alliance members were paying tribute to Athens to protect them from the Persians. This caused great animosity and resentments among the League members and Athens would quell rebellions among League members. Finally open warfare began with the strongest of the other League members, the Spartans. They found a way to overcome the naval advantages of the Athenians and Athens was eventually crushed. The Athenians were strong but they had gotten to the point where they thought they were better than anybody else, more powerful, more triumphant, more naturally worthy of holding and wielding power.

The bigger they are the harder they fall. Sick nations destroy themselves internally or they are destroyed from the outside by the enemies they create in their sickness.

We need to ask ourselves a very crucial question: Is the America we love a sick nation?

After the fall of communism the United States began to take unto itself the role of world policeman. We determined the fate of nations. We forced countries into submission. We toppled dictators and brought minions to power in other countries. We supplied arms to those we decided were in the right, supported insurgents and brought down legitimate authorities who defied or displeased us. We fought wars that were not in our national interest and against countries which had not attacked us, and did not intend to.

We were the world's only superpower. We had the world's most dominate economy. We had the biggest and the most destructive weapons. We had nuclear everything; nuclear tipped rockets, nuclear submarines, nuclear bombers, and we were the only country ever to use a nuclear weapon in war.

Do you think this might have created some resentment overseas? Do you think there might possibly be those who would be delighted to see us suffer and fall? Why did terrorism arise suddenly against Western nations and against our troops, ships and embassies overseas? Why was a great part of the Muslim world ecstatic on 9-11-2001?

Now the sickness is rotting us from the inside out. And the murder of the innocent by a highly militarized police is just the latest excrescence on the body politic.

Our own corporations are deserting the ship in what is called "inversion". A corporation essentially abandons its U.S. citizenship and moves its corporate address to another country while operating almost all of its business within the United States. This is done in the name of serving its shareholders by not paying its fair share of U.S. taxes. Guess who the major shareholders of these corporations are. Yep, it's the super rich who got that way in the first place by exploiting their fellow Americans.

What sicknesses are rotting us from the inside out? Let's talk about a few of them. Hardly any Congressman exists who is not bought and paid for by some agenda driven group implacably motivated by policies blatantly against the public interest.

Our Presidents and Vice-Presidents are international criminals and war mongers, and are not even indicted when they leave office. They retire back to private life immeasurably enriched at the expense of the public and untouched even by very much public shame. Bush and Cheney are of course prime examples. President Obama has seen fit to kill United States citizens without bringing them before a court of justice and without a trial. Drones are just so handy to use.

The United States is far and away the biggest purveyor of war and war making materials that has ever existed on this planet. Our Supreme Court is corrupt and acts as the handmaiden of the super rich, passing such totally destructive opinions as

Citizen United. Declaring that corporations are natural persons and that money is free speech is tantamount to national suicide. Our bankers and money managers from Wall Street to the lowest mortgage brokers steal the very housing from our citizens with total impunity. They suffer little or no consequences after fleecing the country of trillions of dollars. They endanger our national economy and, indeed, the economies of the whole world, and yet they proceed as if nothing is amiss and its business as usual.

Corporate shills and venal congressmen continue to deny the scientifically proven existence of global warming. They are not only endangering the United States for short term monetary gain, but the ability of our species to exist on this planet at all. They block every attempt to take any reasonable steps to move toward environmental protection and alternative energy sources. They come up with patently ridiculous concepts like "clean coal" in order to continue outmoded and dangerous industrial uses, and energy practices. This is truly insane and perhaps the most dangerous policy that a government has ever devised.

The NSA, not content with snooping and surveillance on those who might truly wish harm to our nation, spies on absolutely everybody with no discretion whatsoever. There once was some expectation of privacy in the United States where the government had no business in the doings of ordinary citizens absent any criminal intent or national menace. No more. And anyone who points out their outrageous overreach is subject to intense harassment and possible subversive charges. Even the Congress is spied on! How crazy is that?

Wealth distribution in the United States is inequitable to the extent that most people cannot even imagine it. If you reduce the over 314 million Americans to a representative 100 people, so each person in that group represents one percent of the population, the top guy has 40% of all the wealth in the country. According to the World Bank the total U.S. wealth is 81.8 trillion in 2014 U.S.dollars. The lowest 80 guys have only 7% of all U.S. wealth. That statistic is horrifying in and of itself. As we used to say in my family, "It's enough to piss off the Good Humor Man".

The truth is treated as a completely useless and inconvenient commodity. A fact checking organization, Punditfact, did a study of Fox News and found that 82% of statements made by guests and moderators or anchors on that channel were totally false. A further 10% of their statements were only partially true. Only 8% of everything said on the channel was completely and totally true. It is a mushroom channel – keep them in the dark and feed them bullshit.

A democracy cannot exist when the public is fed an unrelenting constant stream of lies, misinformation, and propaganda, for a voter's judgment is impaired and those who are responsible for political harm are supported and rewarded. Steve Benen, a political fact checker, reported that Mitt Romney knowingly told 533 documented lies in 30 weeks during his unsuccessful presidential campaign in 2012. These were not assertions, interpretations or allegations by Mr. Benen. The falsehoods were factual, all backed up and sourced, actual instances of documented lies by Romney.

So, given all of this sleaze at the highest levels of our government and in our most important national institutions, is it truly surprising that our policing agencies are also involved?

What is the antidote to this national sickness? That is what we need to explore.

YOU - YES YOU! - CAN HELP

What can you do? How can you keep our beloved nation, our precious America, from going the way of Athens, of Japan, of Nazi Germany? How can you prevent the horrendous demise of a truly great nation, the land of the free and once again the home of the brave?

You must be courageous.

You must do what is right for yourself and for your fellow Americans whatever their race, creed, political party or affiliation. You must restore integrity to our national life and our public and private institutions.

How can you do this? It will not be easy but it just may be the most important thing you can do with your life.

You have to start from within. You have to be courageous and honestly examine yourself and determine if you, you personally, are doing the right thing, the honorable thing for yourself, you family, your neighbor, and your fellow American right here and now, today. If you do not operate from the truth who can you expect to do so?

This type of self examination is not easy. It is maybe the toughest thing you have ever done. Who wants to admit they are wrong? Who wants to delve deeply into their own motives for the things they do which cause them a little twinge of the heart? Who wants to make any real change? Act always with integrity? Go the extra mile when it is not strictly required? Be a boy scout or a girl scout?

Americans are not known for this kind of thinking. In fact we may be an utterly superficial nation. We act from self interest and greed and power grabbing and selfishness more than we ever would care to admit.

But, if we are to survive, if we are to carry out the noble spirit on which our nation was founded we must change. We must start with the truth, the truth about ourselves first, and then the truth about our family, the truth about our community, the truth about our State, and the truth about our country.

Once you are really living from your truth and have developed a conscience, you can be a magnet for change. People are irresistibly drawn to a really good person. Think about the best person you personally know. What makes them that way? What do they do that draws other people to them, makes other people feel they want to be around them? You can be that man or woman.

From there you can be a good friend, a good neighbor, a good citizen. You can do something good every day for someone else and try not to get caught doing it. Just one thing each day! It really isn't that hard, but it does take practice and persistence.

Then you can extend a little. You can do the right thing for your community and your country. You don't cheat on your taxes. You vote. Your refuse to vote for anyone no matter what party they belong to who does not tell the truth. You vote in your own best interest. What is the candidate really saying? Who do they represent? You? Or do they represent some sort of special interest?

Any special interest is not good for the country no matter what it is. Why? Because it is seeking an advantage which is unfair to the people not party to that interest. An example is gerrymandering. Gerrymandering is patently immoral and should be made illegal. It is the tool of a corrupt system. It is keeping people in office who should have no place in the public dialogue because they are not interested in the public good. Do not support any political candidate who supports gerrymandering.

Demand that justice be done. If a cop commits a crime he should have no protection from justice, any more than any other criminal. Demand that he be fired and prosecuted and don't stop until he is. Demand that prosecutors do their work impartially. Seek truth and justice in your home and your community.

Work to remove people from office who are corrupt and unjust. It does not matter their political party. Injustice to others will surely and inevitably bring injustice to you. Support and help people who are worse off than you. Give from the abundance that you have been given. Think about the needs of your neighbor and don't abandon them to the spiritually bankrupt wolves now running our political life.

This stuff is not heroic. It is just common sense and good citizenship. More than that, it is just survival. It is survival for you, for your neighbor, your community and for the United States of America.

You may think all of this is simplistic and naïve. Maybe it is. But I think we have to start somewhere and I cannot think of a better place to start than with me. I love America and I want to be the best American possible. Call me a fool and I will own up to it, but I am still going to do it. I hope you will join me.

Thanks for listening. Thanks for being a true American.

AUTHOR BIOGRAPHY

THOMAS EMANUEL is an award winning author and journalist. He holds a Master's degree from Georgetown University. Tom, an accomplished writer and speaker, has written more than 12 books on topics of public interest. He is a voracious reader and loves to travel with his wife.

To learn more about his books, look for his name as an author on Amazon and Kindle. You can contact him by writing to tjepublishing@gmail.com.

The author would really appreciate it if you would write a review of this book on Amazon. Please help to get this book into the hands of those who need it. Thank you.

Printed in the USA
CPSIA information can be obtained
at www.ICGtesting.com
CBHW070822281124
17970CB00053B/658